GREEN PASTURES
Still Waters

31 DAYS IN PSALM 23

Colin S. Smith
with
Tim Augustyn

Scripture quotations are from the ESV® Bible (The Holy Bible, English Standard Version®), copyright © 2001 by Crossway, a publishing ministry of Good News Publishers. Used by permission. All rights reserved.

Copyright © 2024 by Colin S. Smith
First published in United States in 2024

The right of Colin S. Smith to be identified as the Author of this Work has been asserted by him in accordance with the Copyright, Designs and Patents Act 1988.

All rights reserved. No part of this publication may be reproduced, stored in a retrieval system or transmitted in any form or by any means, electronic, mechanical, photocopying, recording or otherwise, without the prior permission of the publisher or the Copyright Licensing Agency.

ISBN: 978-1-7346510-4-1
Design by Breana Rodriguez and typeset by Shannon Hannasch

Published by Open the Bible
PO Box 3454, Barrington, IL 60010
Email: info@openthebible.org
Website: www.openthebible.org

Printed in the United States of America

GREEN PASTURES

Day 1

ALL YOU NEED TO KNOW ABOUT SHEPHERDS

The LORD is my shepherd. Psalm 23:1

STILL WATERS

Many of us live in cities or suburbs, so we don't have firsthand knowledge of what a shepherd is or what a shepherd does. But even if you have never seen a flock of sheep in your life, this psalm tells you all that you need to know about a shepherd.

1. A shepherd **owns** the sheep (23:2). And the Good Shepherd owns us. He says, "*My* sheep… will never perish" (John 10:27-28).

2. A shepherd **leads** the sheep (23:2-3). And the Good Shepherd leads us into rest and into righteousness.

3. A shepherd **restores** the sheep (23:3). And the Good Shepherd retrieves us when we are lost and restores us when we are spent.

4. A shepherd **protects** the sheep (23:4-5). And the Good Shepherd protects us from evil and from enemies.

5. A shepherd **feeds** the sheep (23:5). And the Good Shepherd invites us to His table and presents us with an overflowing cup.

6. A shepherd **loves** the sheep (23:6). And the Good Shepherd loves us with a love that pursues us and will one day welcome us into His presence.

Maybe this feels a bit sentimental to you—fluffy sheep for a children's bedtime story. But there's nothing sentimental about the work of a shepherd. When the lion and the bear came, David stood with the sheep to protect them even at risk to his own life. Now he says, "The Lord is my shepherd. This is how He is with me."

Psalm 23 deals with the realities of life. David had enemies who hunted him, his own son hated him, and he lived under the constant stress of managing an entire nation. He knew about failure and he knew about fear. He knew what it was to be discouraged and exhausted.

When you face difficult decisions, this psalm is for you. When you are losing heart, this psalm is for you. When you face enemies, this psalm is for you. And, since one day you will walk through the valley of death, this psalm is for you. You need a shepherd.

Notes

GREEN PASTURES

Day 2

PSALM 23 IS ABOUT THE LORD

The LORD is my shepherd. PSALM 23:1

In the Old Testament, God appointed prophets, priests, and kings to shepherd His people. Their calling was to feed the sheep, seek the sheep, and guard the sheep. But they didn't do their job.

The quality of life enjoyed by any flock depends entirely on their shepherd. And in Ezekiel's day, the shepherds failed to care for God's sheep: "The weak you have not strengthened, the sick you have not healed, the injured you have not bound up, the strayed you have not brought back, the lost you have not sought, and with force and harshness you have ruled them" (Ezek. 34:4).

So what happened? God said, "I myself will search for my sheep and will seek them out... I will seek the lost, and I will bring back the strayed, and I will bind up the injured, and I will strengthen the weak" (34:11, 16).

And when Jesus came into the world He said, "I am the good shepherd... I know [my sheep]...

I lay down my life for the sheep... [My sheep] will never perish" (John 10:11, 14, 15, 28). All the way through, this psalm is about the Lord.

> *The LORD* is my shepherd…
> *He* makes me lie down in green pastures.
> *He* leads me beside still waters.
> *He* restores my soul.
> *He* leads me in paths of righteousness…
>
> I will fear no evil, for *you* are with me;
> *Your* rod and *your* staff, they comfort me.
> *You* prepare a table before me in the presence of my enemies;
> *You* anoint my head with oil…
> And I shall dwell in the house of *the LORD* forever.

Your experience of life depends on who your shepherd is. David said, "The LORD is my shepherd." And the rest of Psalm 23 shows us what it means to be owned by the Lord: "I am blessed, because He will lead me, restore me, protect me, feed me, and love me."

Notes

GREEN PASTURES

Day 3

YOU WERE BOUGHT WITH A PRICE

You are not your own, for you were bought with a price.
1 CORINTHIANS 6:19-20

STILL WATERS

A shepherd can breed sheep, or he can buy them. A lamb is added to the flock because it is bought or because it is born. And in God's flock both are true. Every Christian has been *bought* into God's flock and every Christian has been *born* into God's flock.

If you are a Christian, this is true of you: "You were ransomed from the futile ways inherited from your forefathers, not with perishable things such as silver or gold, but with the precious blood of Christ, like that of a lamb without blemish or spot" (1 Pet. 1:18-19).

Brothers and sisters in Christ, do you see what the Lord has done for you? He bought you. He paid a price to make you His own.

Maybe you have heard of the television series *This Farming Life*. It's about sheep and cattle farming. Every year farmers go to sheep auctions, where they buy rams for breeding or ewes for growing their flock. And before the auction, the farmers walk around the pens and look at the sheep. They decide which ones they want to buy and how much they want to bid.

The Lord Jesus Christ purchased you and the price He paid was the laying down of His own life.

You are not your own. You have been bought with a price. The Lord is now your shepherd and that is why you will not lack anything. "The LORD is my shepherd; I shall not want" (Psa. 23:1).

What you need will be given to you because the Shepherd has made you His own. Since He gave Himself to purchase you, you can be sure that He will give you all that you need (Rom. 8:32).

Notes

GREEN PASTURES

Day 4

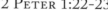
YOU WERE BORN INTO GOD'S FLOCK

Love one another earnestly from a pure heart, since you have been born again, not of perishable seed but of imperishable, through the living and abiding word of God.
2 PETER 1:22-23

STILL WATERS

You have been bought into Christ's flock, *and* you have been born into His flock. For sheep it would be one or the other, but both are true of you.

The Spirit of God moved over your dead soul just as He moved over the dark and dead waters in the beginning. He brought you to life. He awakened you to your need for a Savior, and He opened your eyes to the glory of Christ. He brought you to faith and gave you a new desire to leave sin and to follow Jesus.

Not only did He bring you to new life, He sustains you in this new life. For all your doubts and fears, for all your unanswered questions, for all your many sins and failings, you still love Christ, and the Lord is still your shepherd.

Having bought or bred the flock, a shepherd lives with his sheep. They are the constant focus of his care and attention. When you belong to the flock of God, you can say with confidence…

The LORD is *my* shepherd…
He makes *me* lie down in green pastures.
He leads *me* beside still waters.
He restores *my* soul.
He leads *me* in paths of righteousness for his name's sake.

Even though *I* walk through the valley of the shadow of death, *I* will fear no evil, for you are with *me*; your rod and your staff, they comfort *me*.
You prepare a table before *me* in the presence of *my* enemies; you anoint *my* head with oil; *my* cup overflows.
Surely goodness and mercy shall follow *me* all the days of my life, and *I* shall dwell in the house of the LORD forever.

Notes

GREEN PASTURES

Day 5

YOU BELONG TO THE SHEPHERD

The good shepherd lays down his life for the sheep. He who is a hired hand and not a shepherd, who does not own the sheep, sees the wolf coming and leaves the sheep and flees.
JOHN 10:11-12

STILL WATERS

The relationship of a shepherd to the sheep is first and foremost one of ownership. The shepherd owns the flock. You may be asking, *Do I want to be wholly owned?* Something in us rebels against that idea.

Back in the garden of Eden, Satan tempted Eve by saying to her, "You will be like God" (Gen. 3:5). And something within the sinful nature persists in believing that life would be different, if only we could take the place of God ourselves.

A popular actress once said, "I know that I exist, therefore I am. I know that the god-source exists, therefore it is. Since I am part of that force, then I am that I am." It's hard not to feel sorry for her and others who think this way. If you are god, you're alone. You have no one to look to but yourself.

When Jesus saw the crowds, He had compassion on them for "they were like sheep without a shepherd" (Mark 6:34). Sheep without a shepherd soon wander off and get lost. And wolves come and destroy them.

The worst that can happen to sheep without a shepherd is that they die. But the worst that will happen to sinners who choose to be their own god is not that they die, it is that ahead of them stretches a dark hell in which they are completely alone.

But David can say, "The Lord is my shepherd. My shepherd *owns* me. His goodness and mercy will follow me all the days of my life. When I die, my shepherd will welcome me home. I will dwell in His house forever." What a marvelous thing it is to be wholly owned by the Son of God.

Notes

GREEN PASTURES

Day 6

WHEN THE LORD IS YOUR SHEPHERD

Then all the tribes of Israel came to David at Hebron and said, "Behold, we are your bone and flesh. In times past, when Saul was king over us, it was you who led out and brought in Israel. And the LORD said to you, 'You shall be shepherd of my people Israel.'"
2 SAMUEL 5:1-2

STILL WATERS

David grew up as a shepherd, but God called him to be a king. And, as the king, David was called to shepherd the people of God. How could he do that? How could *he* lead God's people? How could *he* restore them, protect them, feed them, and love them?

And here is David's answer: "The Lord is *my* shepherd. What God has called me to do for others, He will do for me."

Think about your own life. How are you going to carry the weight of responsibility that is on you? You may have great responsibilities at home or at work. The decisions you make will affect the lives of others. How are you going to discharge your duties?

You can shepherd others because God will shepherd you. You will be able to restore and refresh others because the Lord will restore and refresh you. You will be able to provide for others because the Lord will provide for you. You will be able to keep loving others because the Lord will never stop loving you. *The Lord is my shepherd; I shall not want.* This is the logic of faith.

You may face hard decisions when you don't know the right way, but the Lord is your shepherd.

He will lead you in right paths. You may be struck down by disease, and laid low without strength, but the Lord is your shepherd. He will restore your soul. You may have enemies who will oppose you and even try to destroy you, but the Lord is your shepherd. He will protect you.

One day you will face the dark valley of death. But the Lord is your shepherd. He will walk with you and bring you safely through. When the Lord is your shepherd, you have all that you need.

Notes

GREEN PASTURES

Day 7

THE SHEPHERD LEADS US INTO REST

He makes me lie down in green pastures. He leads me beside still waters. He restores my soul.
PSALM 23:2, 3

STILL WATERS

The first blessing of being wholly owned by the Good Shepherd is that He leads us. David says this twice. "He leads me beside still waters… He leads me in paths of righteousness for his name's sake" (23:3).

Notice that David states this as a fact, a given. Here is what the shepherd does. There is nothing you have to do in order to make this happen. If you are in the flock of God, this is true of you. This is what He does for you—He leads you. Paul puts it this way in the New Testament: "All who are led by the Spirit of God are sons of God" (Rom. 8:14).

Where does He lead us? The first place He leads us is into rest: "He makes me lie down in green pastures. He leads me beside still waters" (Psa. 23:2). Green pastures provide grazing for the sheep.

But the main point here is not feeding but resting. "He makes me *lie down* in green pastures."

Then David says, "He leads me beside still waters" (23:2). Sheep are scared of moving water.

If the sheep fell into the water, their fleece would soak up the water like a sponge, and the weight would cause them to drown. So, a good shepherd will dam up a river and make a place where the water is still so that the sheep can drink.

David gives us two beautiful descriptions of rest to stir up our imaginations—first, the meadow with its lush grass; and second, pools of still water.

Notes

GREEN PASTURES

Day 8

SHEEP DO NOT NATURALLY OR EASILY FIND REST

*In peace I will both lie down and sleep; for you alone,
O LORD, make me dwell in safety.*
PSALM 4:8

STILL WATERS

Sheep are timid creatures and the only way they can defend themselves is to run, so they stay on their feet. How can sheep lie down when they are so vulnerable?

Maybe you find it hard to rest. You have a problem to solve or a challenge to face, and you have many fears. Your mind will not rest. You lie awake at night, going over all that has happened, and all that could happen. You need rest, but you don't know how to find it.

David found it difficult to rest too—being on the run from Saul, worrying about his divided and dysfunctional family, and carrying the weight of responsibility as a king. Rest did not come easily or naturally to him, but David said, "The Lord… *makes me* lie down" (23:2).

Imagine you are in a flock of sheep. When you can see your shepherd, you lie down and rest. If the wolf comes, the shepherd is there. He will deal with the wolf. But if the shepherd were to leave, you would quickly get up on your feet, watching for danger, ready to run.

David says, "My shepherd… makes me lie down." And here's how: "Even though I walk through the valley of the shadow of death, I will fear no evil, for you are with me" (23:4). Even if you go through death, you have nothing to fear, because your Shepherd is with you, and when you know He is with you, you will be able to rest.

The shepherd does not give rest to the sheep by ridding the world of danger. The wolves are still out there. The sheep lie down because they can see the shepherd. His presence gives them rest.

You can face your fears today by reminding yourself, "I do not face this alone. The Shepherd is with me. And my Shepherd is the Lord God Almighty!"

Notes

GREEN PASTURES

Day 9

THE SHEPHERD LEADS US ON RIGHT PATHS

He leads me in paths of righteousness.
PSALM 23:3

"Paths of righteousness" simply means the right paths. Where the Shepherd leads you will always be the right path. But the right path will not always be an easy path. In verse 5, the right path takes you through the presence of enemies. In verse 4, the right path takes you through the valley of the shadow of death. But even there the Good Shepherd will lead you.

The Gospels record an occasion when Jesus said to His disciples: "Let us go across to the other side [of the lake]" (Mark 4:35). Then Jesus got into a boat and led the disciples into a storm. But it was in the storm that they saw His glory and learned that they could trust Him.

Sometimes the Good Shepherd will lead you through the waters, like He did at the Red Sea: "Your way was through the sea, your path through the great waters; yet your footprints were unseen. You led your people like a flock by the hand of Moses and Aaron" (Psa. 77:19-20).

There will be times when the way God leads you seems impossible. When God's people came to the Red Sea, it seemed that there was no way forward. But God made a way through, and He said, "When you pass through the waters, I will be with you" (Isa. 43:2).

There will be times when you can't feel the presence of God. When God's people crossed the Red Sea, God was leading them, guarding them, and with them, yet His footprints were unseen.

There will be times when you say, "Where is God in this? I can't see Him." God's ways may be a mystery to you, but when the Lord is your Shepherd, He will lead you.

There will be times when God's direction comes through other people. "You led your people like a flock by the hand of Moses and Aaron" (Psa. 77:20). Seek the wisdom and counsel of others when you are trying to discern the right path. This is one of the ways God will lead you, and one reason why He puts other believers around you.

Notes

GREEN PASTURES

Day 10

WHEN THE SHEPHERD MOVES YOU

He leads me in paths of righteousness.
PSALM 23:3

STILL WATERS

When sheep are put into a field of lush grass, they enjoy a feast. The problem is that they don't know when to stop. And if they are left in a field for too long, they will eat not only the grass, but the roots too, and they will leave the field completely barren.

So, before the field gets overgrazed, a good shepherd will move his sheep on to the next field. He moves them so that he can nourish them somewhere else. Knowing this will help you when you face change in your life.

Here is something that all of us will face at some point. God will put you in a place where the grass is green. You are happy in the field, and when the Shepherd moves you on, you don't want to go. "Why can't I stay here longer? I don't want to leave this field."

But when the Shepherd chooses to move you, He is saying to you, "This is no longer the place where you will be nourished. I have another place where I will provide for you. There I will feed you. There I will make you lie down. Do not be afraid. This is the right path."

You may not want to move to the field where the Shepherd leads you, but He will feed you there. He will feed you in a way that your soul would not have been fed if you had stayed where you were before. So, trust the Shepherd when He chooses to move you.

Notes

GREEN PASTURES

Day 11

WHY THE SHEPHERD WILL NEVER GIVE UP ON YOU

He leads me in paths of righteousness for his name's sake.
PSALM 23:3

When you come to a dark valley, you may find yourself saying, "I feel like giving up on myself. How do I know God won't give up on me?" The answer lies in the words "for his name's sake."

The apostle Paul tells us that he was a blasphemer and a violent man (1 Tim. 1:13). But then he says, "I received mercy for this reason, that in me, as the foremost, Jesus Christ might display his perfect patience" (1:16). In other words, "God picked the worst of people to show how patient He is. God did not choose me because He saw something lovable in me."

You may say, "I like to think that when God looks at me, He sees something beautiful. He is drawn to me because of what He sees in me. He loves because I'm lovable."

But where would that leave you when you are no longer beautiful? Where would you be when what God sees in you is not attractive, but ugly? What would become of you when, in your persistent and tiresome waywardness, you are far from lovable?

The good news is that God does not lead you for your sake. God leads you for His name's sake. The Good Shepherd has staked His own name and reputation on leading you safely home. His grace, His patience, and His faithfulness will be put on display forever through what He will make of you. That is why He will never give up on you.

No angel in heaven will ever say, "It's a shame that sheep was too weak to make it. What a pity that one wandered off and never came home." No. God has given His word. Every sheep in His flock will be brought safely home. Not one of them will be missing.

The Good Shepherd has staked His name on leading you home. Despite your many sins and wanderings, despite the enemies that assault you and the doubts that assail you, you will arrive safely home. The honor of the Shepherd's name hangs on it.

Notes

GREEN PASTURES

Day 12

WE DON'T FIND IT EASY TO FOLLOW

The LORD is my shepherd… He restores my soul.
PSALM 23:1, 3

STILL WATERS

At some point in your life, you will need each verse of this psalm. But these four words are the most wonderful of all: "He restores my soul." David is saying, "God has restored me many times in the past and He will restore me many times in the future as well."

Why is this so important? Why do we need it? If the Shepherd leads the sheep, surely that is all that we need? Why would we ever need restoring? Because, although the Shepherd leads us, we often go astray. And when we go astray, we don't know how to find our way back.

God led His people in the wilderness. He made Himself visibly present in a pillar of cloud by day and a pillar of fire by night. All they had to do was to follow. But you know the story—they grumbled and complained. In their hearts, they wanted to go back to Egypt. And when they were about to enter the Promised Land, their faith faltered.

Here's the problem: The Lord leads His people, but we don't find it easy to follow. You know this contradiction in your own life. You love the Lord but your heart wanders, your obedience falters, your faith often burns low. And if your final salvation depended on the consistency of your following the Shepherd, you would never arrive safely home.

God uses the image of sheep to describe His own people. Believers wander. "All we like sheep have gone astray; we have turned—every one—to his own way; and the Lord has laid on him the iniquity of us all" (Isa. 53:6).

The same is true in the parable of the prodigal son. The prodigal is a son, and he belongs to the father. Yet there is also something in him that pulls away from the father.

This is our position as Christian believers. We are God's flock. We belong to the Father. We are redeemed by the blood of Christ. We are new creations. And yet, there remains within us an impulse to wander. So, thank God for this wonderful truth—*He restores my soul*.

Notes

GREEN PASTURES

Day 13

WHY WE ARE PRONE TO WANDER

I have been crucified with Christ. It is no longer I who live, but Christ who lives in me. And the life I now live in the flesh I live by faith in the Son of God, who loved me and gave himself for me. GALATIANS 2:20

Notice the twin realities of Christian experience. We live *by faith* in the Son of God, but we live this life of faith *in the flesh*.

Here's why we are prone to wander: The Spirit has given us new life, but we live this life in the flesh. God's saving work in us has begun, but it is not yet complete. We are not yet what we will be. Only when we see Christ will we be fully like Him.

This is why Paul speaks of Christians as "us who are being saved" (1 Cor. 1:18). This is present tense—we are being saved. The process is ongoing. And until the day when we arrive safely home, we have it in us to wander.

Octavius Winslow said, "If there is one consideration more humbling than another to a spiritually-minded believer, it is, that, after all God has done for him,…there should still exist in the heart a principle, the tendency of which is to secret, perpetual, and alarming departure from God."

That is the reality of Christian experience, and David knew it. David had a heart after God, and yet there were desires in his heart that overwhelmed this love and dragged him into self-destructive sins.

If it were not for the truth we are looking at today, that would have been the end for David, and our sins would have been the end for us too. But here's the good news: The Good Shepherd retrieves us when we wander. *He restores my soul.*

Notes

GREEN PASTURES

Day 14

HOW YOUR LOVE FOR JESUS CAN BE RESTORED

"I know your works, your toil and your patient endurance, and how you cannot bear with those who are evil, but have tested those who call themselves apostles and are not, and found them to be false. I know you are enduring patiently and bearing up for my name's sake, and you have not grown weary. But I have this against you, that you have abandoned the love you had at first." REVELATION 2:2-4

These were good people—hardworking, upright, discerning, and loyal. But Jesus said, "I have this against you, that you have abandoned the love you had at first" (2:4).

If you lose your first love for Christ, how do you get it back? David tells us: "[The Lord] restores my soul" (Psa. 23:3). He does it by reminding us of what we have lost: "Remember therefore from where you have fallen" (Rev. 2:5).

Restoration begins with an honest recognition of what has been lost. Your heart has become cold. You were not always like this. The truth is that you have gone backwards. You have lost ground. Better things were once true of you and better things can be true of you again.

Remembering from where you have fallen will lead you to repent. The prodigal son had a kind and loving father, yet he wandered away and squandered what had been given to him. He wasted his time, his money, and his strength. But then he remembered, "My father's hired servants have more than enough bread, but I perish here with hunger!" (Luke 15:17). So, he said, "I will arise and go to my father" (15:18).

Remembering leads to repenting. And God restores us, by reminding us what we have lost. In God's kindness, may this happen for you today: "That's exactly what I need! I've lost my peace and joy. I've lost my first love for Christ, and I need Him to restore my soul."

You can ask the Good Shepherd to do this for you. That's what David did. He remembered the joy and he asked God to give it back: "Restore to me the joy of your salvation" (Psa. 51:12).

Notes

GREEN PASTURES

Day 15

THE SHEPHERD RESTORES US WHEN WE FALTER

He restores my soul. Psalm 23:3

STILL WATERS

Sometimes we need to be restored because we wandered away from the Shepherd. The root of the problem lay in our own sin and folly. But there is more to God's work of restoration than retrieving us when we wander.

Phillip Keller worked for many years as a shepherd, and wrote a book called *A Shepherd Looks at Psalm 23.* He describes a condition in which a sheep becomes *cast*. This can happen when the sheep's fleece is long and heavy, or when it is carrying lambs.

The problem, in either case, is the weight that the sheep carries. If a sheep lies down on its side, all is well. But if it rolls onto its back, it will soon be in trouble. It cannot right itself, and it lies there helpless with four feet kicking in the air.

When a sheep is on its back, it cannot restore itself. Keller says, "As it lies there struggling, gases begin to build up in the rumen. As these expand they tend to retard and cut off blood circulation to extremities of the body, especially the legs."

He describes how, as a shepherd, he would restore a cast sheep. "I would have to lift her onto her feet, then straddling the sheep with my legs I would hold her erect, rubbing her limbs to restore the circulation to her legs. This often took quite a little time. When the sheep started to walk again she often just stumbled, staggered and collapsed in a heap once more… [But] little by little the sheep would regain its equilibrium."

There are many examples of faltering in the Bible: Faith can falter when we are disoriented by injustice. "My feet had almost stumbled, my steps had nearly slipped." (Psa. 73:2);

Faith can falter when we are drained by conflict. "I, even I only, am left." (1 Kings 19:10); Faith can falter when we are disappointed by outcomes. "Let us not grow weary in doing good." (Gal. 6:9); Faith can falter when we are disheartened by suffering. "You endured a hard struggle with sufferings." (Heb. 10:32); Faith can falter when we are depleted by demands. "Who is sufficient for these things." (2 Cor. 2:16); Asaph in Psalm 73, Elijah in 1 Kings 19, the Galatian church, the Hebrews, and the apostle Paul in 2 Corinthians 2: They all faltered and they were all restored.

Notes

GREEN PASTURES

Day 16

THE SHEPHERD IS ABLE TO RESTORE YOU

The LORD is my shepherd… He restores my soul.
PSALM 23:1, 3

We don't restore ourselves. God restores us. And He restores us through a fresh encounter in which God Himself draws near.

God may surprise you by how He comes alongside you and lifts you. He has many means of doing this, but of this you can be sure: when the Lord is your shepherd, He will restore your soul.

God is able to restore you. God gave life to your soul. He is able to restore life to your soul. He made you alive in Christ. He is able to keep you alive in Christ.

When God restores you, He will do it gently. David said, "Your gentleness made me great" (Psa. 18:35). Think of the shepherd rubbing the legs of the cast sheep. There is patience, tenderness, and perseverance. God will restore you gently and joyfully. The shepherd himself goes after the wandering sheep, puts it on His shoulders, and brings it home "rejoicing" (Luke 15:5).

When your faith is faltering and the Shepherd finds you,

He will not rebuke you. He has come looking for you. He has come to restore you. And God finds great joy in restoring His own.

Think about this. How is it, that after all you have endured in your life, you are still a Christian today? With all the injustice that is around you, with all the conflict you have endured, with all the disappointments you have encountered, with all the pain you have suffered, with all the demands that are upon you? After all that, how are you still a believer today?

There's only one explanation. He restores your soul. God's restoration explains your continuing in the faith. And God's restoration guarantees your arrival in glory.

Notes

GREEN PASTURES

Day 17

THE SHADOW OF DEATH

Even though I walk through the valley of the shadow of death... Psalm 23:4

STILL WATERS

Death casts a shadow. David is describing what leads up to death—the prospect of death, what comes before it, the dawning realization that we are going to go into this valley and there is no way we can avoid it.

Christians sometimes say, "It's not death that scares me. It's the process of dying. It's what I might have to go through to get there." Why would we say that?

If you belong to the flock of God, the moment of your death will be the most glorious experience you have ever enjoyed. Suddenly, you will be away from the body and at home with the Lord. This world, with all of its pain and conflict, with all of its tears and sorrow, will be behind you. At last you will see face to face the One you have loved and trusted.

If you are in Christ, death itself will be glorious for you. But getting there is an entirely different thing—your body declining, your world contracting, your control of what is happening around you diminishing. It is not the valley itself that frightens us. It's the shadow that lies before it.

And that is what David is talking about here.

Death is not the only valley that casts a shadow over us. Dying is the last valley, but there are other valleys that we walk through on the way—the dark valley of depression, the dark valley of unemployment, the dark valley of a business failure or a painful lawsuit, the dark valley of a serious illness or of caring for someone who becomes increasingly dependent on you.

Every Christian knows what it is to walk through times of darkness, and when you find yourself in a dark valley, this psalm is for you.

Notes

GREEN PASTURES

Day 18

THE SHEPHERD IS WITH YOU EVEN IN THE DARKNESS

Even though I walk through the valley of the shadow of death… you are with me. PSALM 23:4

STILL WATERS

You may know what this is like—a great darkness falls on you, and you wonder if God has deserted you. But David said, "You are with me" (23:4).

There is a remarkable story in Exodus 19-20, when God came down on Mount Sinai to give the Ten Commandments. The mountain was covered in darkness; it was shaking like an earthquake. There was thunder and lightning. Even Moses said, "I tremble with fear" (Heb. 12:21).

Then God spoke the Ten Commandments in an audible voice: *You shall have no other gods before me. Honor your father and your mother. You shall not murder. You shall not steal. You shall not covet.* The people were afraid and said to Moses, "You speak to us, and we will listen; but do not let God speak to us, lest we die" (Ex. 20:19). So, Moses climbed the mountain, and we read these words: "Moses drew near to the thick darkness where God was" (Ex. 20:21).

When you find yourself in a time of great darkness you may not be able to feel the presence of God. Jesus hung on the cross, and for three hours He was plunged into absolute darkness. In the darkness, He cried out in a loud voice, "My God, My God, why have you forsaken me?" (Mat. 27:45-46). No one ever knew the love of God the Father like God the Son, but in that darkness, when He bore our sins, Jesus could no longer feel the comfort of His Father's love.

Was the Father there in the darkness of the cross? Yes, He was. What was He doing? God was reconciling the world to Himself in Christ (2 Cor. 5:19). God is with you in the darkness as much as He is with you in the light.

Notes

GREEN PASTURES

Day 19

WHAT LIES BEYOND DEATH FOR YOU

I will fear no evil, for you are with me. PSALM 23:4

STILL WATERS

Our Lord entered the shadow of death in Gethsemane where He prayed: "My Father, if it be possible, let this cup pass from me" (Mat. 26:39). Jesus knew He had to go through the dark valley of death, but He could say to the Father, "I will fear no evil, for you are with me."

The Bible speaks about death in two ways—the *first* and the *second* death. The *first* death is death as we know it—physical death, where the soul is separated from the body. The *second* death is the judgment of God that will be poured out on the last day (Rev. 20:6, 14).

Jesus experienced the first death and the second death at the same time. Wicked men nailed Him to the cross, and over six hours, life drained from His body. And, at the same time, God laid our sins on Jesus and poured out the judgment that was due to us on Him.

The death of Jesus has changed death for all who belong to Him. So, when you enter the first death, what lies ahead on the other side is not the second death. What lies beyond death for you is a glorious entrance into the presence of God.

That's why Paul can say, "O death, where is your victory? O death where is your sting?" (1 Cor. 15:55). Christian believers will never taste the second death. Jesus endured it for us and drew its sting. Your death, when it comes, will not be an entrance into judgment but into everlasting joy.

Death will separate you from your work. It will separate you from your loved ones. It will separate you from your own body. But it can never separate you from the love of Christ.

Notes

GREEN PASTURES

Day 20

WHEN YOU PASS THROUGH THE VALLEY OF DEATH

Even though I walk through the valley of the shadow of death, I will fear no evil, for you are with me; your rod and your staff, they comfort me. PSALM 23:4

STILL WATERS

The rod was a club carried by the shepherd to fend off wild animals that might attack the sheep. The staff is the shepherd's crook that he uses to lift the lambs up into his arms. So, the rod and staff speak of the strength and the love of the Good Shepherd.

However dark the valley may be, you do not need to fear because the Lord is with you. No power can snatch you from His hand. Nothing can separate you from His love. What will it be like when you pass through the valley of death?

The disciples were alone in a boat on a lake at night, the wind was against them, and they were straining at the oars. Then, in the middle of the night, Jesus went out to meet them, walking on the water.

Imagine the disciples looking out into the darkness—seeing this figure walking toward them on the water. Mark records, "When they saw him walking on the sea they thought it was a ghost" (Mark 6:49). When they saw Him, they were *terrified*. But Jesus said, "Take heart; it is I. Do not be afraid" (6:50).

That is a marvelous picture of what happens to the believer at the moment of death. You have been straining at the oars. The wind has been against you. You find yourself in a dark place and you feel that your own life is slipping away from you.

Do not be afraid. Here is what happens for a believer at the moment of death. Jesus comes to take you home. He will come to you as He came to the disciples in the darkness: "Take heart; It is I. Do not be afraid." And then, before you know it, you will be on the other side—no more wind, no more darkness, no more straining at the oars.

Notes

GREEN PASTURES

Day 21

THE SHEPHERD SUSTAINS YOU BY GIVING YOU STRENGTH

You prepare a table before me in the presence of my enemies. PSALM 23:5

STILL WATERS

Take in this scene. You arrive home after a hard day at work. Someone is in the kitchen cooking. You say, "Let me help." But this person says, "Sit down. Let me prepare this for you."

So, you sit down and watch as this person prepares a meal *before* you. When it is done, you come to the table, and as you eat, your strength is renewed. That's the picture.

Here's the question. Who would do that for you? David says that the person who does this for him is the Lord Himself!

Notice, this is present tense. It is not something God did a long time ago. It is not something God does once in a while. It is what God is always doing for His people.

God uses this picture to tell you that He will sustain you by giving you strength. As your body is strengthened by a good meal, you will be sustained as the Lord Himself feeds you.

But there is something else here: "You prepare a table before me *in the presence of my enemies*" (23:5).

David's life was an unrelenting battle. In his early years, he was a shepherd, despised by his older brothers. Then he lived as a fugitive, hunted by King Saul. When he became king, he inherited a divided kingdom, where rival tribes were filled with resentment and distrust.

In his later years, David suffered as his family was torn apart by cycles of abuse, violence, and death. At one point, he had to flee for his life when his own son led a rebellion against him.

How in the world did David keep going? How will *you* keep going in the light of the many pressures, burdens, conflicts, and troubles of *your* life?

God prepared a table for David. He renewed David's strength even in the presence of his enemies. And what God did for David, He can do for you.

Notes

GREEN PASTURES

Day 22

THE SHEPHERD SUSTAINS YOU BY GIVING YOU PURPOSE

You anoint my head with oil. Psalm 23:5

Oil was used in the Old Testament to commission certain people for the work God had called them to do. Prophets, priests, and kings were all anointed with oil because God had given them a particular assignment. If the table speaks of new strength, the oil speaks of new purpose.

There is a beautiful description of how Aaron was anointed with oil as a sign that God had chosen Him to serve as high priest: "Behold, how good and pleasant it is when brothers dwell in unity! It is like the precious oil on the head, running down on the beard, on the beard of Aaron, running down on the collar of his robes!" (Psa. 133:1, 2).

This was not a little oil rubbed onto Aaron's forehead. The anointing oil was poured out over his head. It ran over his beard, dripped onto his collar, and soaked into his robes.

When David says, "You anoint my head with oil," he must surely have had in mind the day he was anointed king: "Samuel took the horn of oil and anointed him in the midst of his brothers. And the Spirit of the LORD rushed upon David from that day forward" (1 Sam. 16:13).

The oil speaks of God giving purpose, a calling, an assignment. In the Old Testament, only a few people were anointed with oil. But in the New Testament, all of God's people are anointed with the Holy Spirit.

A sense of purpose sustained David: "God has given me this work to do. I've been called. I've been anointed." If you lose sight of why you are here and what God has called you to do, you will soon be tired, jaded, drained, and spent.

But God has work for you to do. "For we are his workmanship, created in Christ Jesus for good works, which God prepared beforehand, that we should walk in them" (Eph. 2:10).

Find out what God has called you to do and pursue it. And as you do, God will sustain you.

Notes

GREEN PASTURES

Day 23

THE SHEPHERD SUSTAINS YOU BY GIVING YOU JOY

My cup overflows. PSALM 23:5

STILL WATERS

There is a version of Christianity that goes like this: In this world you will be surrounded by enemies, but you have to get through this. And if you do, you will be blessed in the end. When your life in this world is over *then* you will have joy. Life stinks, but heaven is coming.

But that is not what David is saying here. He knew plenty of trouble in his life, and yet he says, "My cup overflows—here in this fallen world, with all that I face and all that I suffer, even now while my enemies are still present, even here in the dark valley."

Jesus said, "In this world you will have [trouble]" (John 16:33). But He also said, "These things I have spoken to you, that my joy may be in you, and that your joy may be full" (John 15:11).

From the fullness of the grace of Jesus we have received one blessing on top of another. His grace just keeps coming. It overflows.

- When Isaiah describes God's forgiveness, it is not enough for him to say that God will pardon. He says that God will *abundantly pardon* (Isa. 55:7).
- When the psalmist describes God's hope, it is not enough for him to say that with God there is redemption. He says that with the Lord there is *plentiful redemption* (Psa. 130:7).
- Paul speaks not just of the riches, but of the *unsearchable riches* of Christ (Eph. 3:8).
- Jesus speaks about giving us not just life, but *abundant life* (John 10:10).

When the prodigal son returned home, the father did not meet him with reluctant grace: "You've decided to come back? Better make sure you don't mess up again." No. The father ran out to meet him, embraced him, kissed him, put the best robe on his back and a ring on his finger.

The father did not say, "There's a cold hot dog in the fridge." He said, "Bring the fattened calf and kill it, and let us eat and celebrate." That's what David experienced. "My cup overflows!"

Notes

GREEN PASTURES

Day 24

HOW STRENGTH, PURPOSE, AND JOY BECOME YOURS

Blessed be the God and Father of our Lord Jesus Christ, who has blessed us in Christ with every spiritual blessing in the heavenly places. EPHESIANS 1:3

David had strength, purpose, and joy. But how can these things become ours? Answer: we are blessed with every spiritual blessing in Christ Jesus.

What did the table mean for Jesus?

On the night He was betrayed, Jesus "reclined at *table* with the twelve" (Mat. 26:20). Jesus took the bread and broke it, as He had when He fed the crowd. But this time He said, "Take, eat; this is my body" (Mat. 26:26). Jesus does more than prepare the meal. He *is* the meal. Jesus said, "I am the bread of life" (John 6:35, 48). "Whoever feeds on me… will live because of me" (John 6:57). You feed on Him by believing in Him.

What did the anointing mean for Jesus?

One day Mary, the sister of Lazarus (whom Jesus raised from the dead), wanted to show her love for Him, so she broke a jar of expensive ointment and poured it over His head (John 12:1-3). Jesus said, "She has *anointed* my body beforehand for burial" (Mark 14:8). Dying was the work the Father had called Him to do, so that you could be appointed to eternal life (Acts 13:48). He died so that you might live. And He anoints His own with the presence and power of the Holy Spirit so that you may be equipped to do the work God has prepared for you.

What did the cup mean for Jesus?

Jesus prayed in the garden of Gethsemane: "My Father, if it be possible, let this *cup* pass from me" (Mat. 26:39). What was this cup? We are told in a description of the final judgment: "The wine of God's wrath, poured full strength into the cup of His anger" (Rev. 14:10). Why did Jesus have to drink this cup? Because "all we like sheep have gone astray… and the Lord has laid on Him the iniquity of us all" (Isa. 53:6). The wrath of divine justice that should have been ours, fell on Jesus. He drank the cup of God's wrath so that you may drink the cup of God's blessing.

Notes

GREEN PASTURES

Day 25

THE SHEPHERD'S INVITATION

My sheep hear my voice... and they follow me.
JOHN 10:27

Perhaps you are not yet a believer. You've heard the claims of Jesus, but you've been brushing them off: "I'm not ready. It's not for me. I don't need this."

You hear that the Good Shepherd leads His sheep into rest. You hear that He restores His sheep when they wander. You hear that He guards His sheep and that He walks with them through the valley of death. You hear that He sustains His sheep by giving them strength and purpose and joy. Isn't there something in you that says, "I would like these things to be true of me?"

Isn't there something in you that would like to be able to say, "The Lord is my shepherd, and I shall not want because He leads me, restores me, guards me, and sustains me"? Jesus came into the world to gather a flock and make them His own. Why should you not be among them?

If you find a desire in your heart for the leading, restoring, guarding, and sustaining that the Good Shepherd does for all of His sheep, you have every reason to thank God: "No one can come to me unless the Father who sent me draws him" (John 6:44).

The Good Shepherd is inviting you to find strength at His table. He is holding the oil, ready to anoint you for a new purpose. He is offering the cup of blessing so that your joy may be full. Jesus says, "My sheep hear my voice," and when you hear the voice of the Good Shepherd, there's only one way to respond. And that is to follow Him.

Give up being self-owned and self-directed. Submit yourself to the Good Shepherd. He will give you new strength, new purpose, and new joy. Begin a new life today in which you follow the Good Shepherd. Give yourself to Him—believe Him, trust Him, obey Him, follow Him.

Notes

GREEN PASTURES

Day 26

REMEMBER ALL THAT THE SHEPHERD DOES FOR YOU

Bless the LORD, O my soul, and forget not all his benefits.
Psalm 103:2

STILL WATERS

Picture what it was like for David to write this psalm under the inspiration of the Holy Spirit. His life was troubled by aggravation from Saul, opposition from the Philistines, the pressures of leading a divided nation, trouble in his own family, and the sins that plagued his own heart.

As David thinks about all that he is facing, his mind goes back to the early years of his life when his work had been keeping the sheep, and some words come to him: *The LORD is my shepherd.*

He thinks about what that means: "When I cared for the sheep, they lacked nothing, and the Lord is a better shepherd than I was, so the same will be true for me." *I shall not want.*

Words continue to come to David as he thinks about what it means for the Lord to be his shepherd. *The Lord leads me.* "He leads me into rest, and He leads me into righteousness."

The Lord restores me. "My heart wanders and my spirit falters. But the Lord picks me up. The Lord brings me back. The Lord will never let me go."

The Lord guards me. "I have walked through some dark valleys and more lie ahead of me. But even when I walk through the darkest valley, my shepherd will be with me."

The Lord sustains me. "The Philistines hate me. Trusted friends betray me. Members of my own family rise up against me. But the Lord stands with me and gives me strength. He prepares a table before me in the presence of my enemies."

This psalm is a meditation on what the Good Shepherd does for His sheep. And David's faith is strengthened as he takes in what the Lord does for him. His first thought was: *I shall not want.* But by the end, he is able to say something better: *Surely goodness and mercy will follow me all the days of my life and I shall dwell in the house of the Lord forever.*

Notes

GREEN PASTURES

Day 27

THE SHEPHERD HAS TWO SHEEPDOGS

Surely goodness and mercy shall follow me all the days of my life. PSALM 23:6

STILL WATERS

A shepherd who once preached on Psalm 23:6 said: "Think of a shepherd walking in front of his sheep. The sheep follow him, and behind them are two sheepdogs chasing after the stragglers and keeping the flock close to the shepherd.

The Good Shepherd has two sheepdogs: one is called *Goodness*; the other is called *Mercy*. What a picture! The Good Shepherd will keep you close to Himself through His goodness and mercy that are always chasing after you.

Goodness

You could easily list many things that are not as you would want them to be. Sin has brought its devastating effects into the world, and things are not as they should be in our world, our country, our work, our churches, our homes, or in our own hearts. But there is good in your life too.

James said, "Every good gift and every perfect gift is from above, coming down from the Father of lights, with whom there is no variation or shadow due to change" (Jas. 1:17). Every good thing in your life comes from God's loving hands, so thank Him. Sinners blame God for everything and thank Him for nothing; believers thank God for everything and blame Him for nothing. If you belong to the Good Shepherd, God's goodness is always chasing after you.

Mercy

Goodness is God giving us what we don't deserve. Mercy is God not giving us what we do deserve. God chases after us with mercy. That is good news, because if God chased after us in justice, we would all be in trouble.

The Bible uses an awful picture to describe God's judgment of the wicked: "As fire consumes the forest, as the flame sets the mountain ablaze" (Psa. 83:14). That's how God's judgment pursues the wicked, like a wildfire consuming everything in its path.

If God was chasing after you with judgment and condemnation, of course you would run. But why would you run when you are being chased by goodness and mercy? "God's kindness is meant to lead you to repentance" (Rom. 2:4). God's goodness and mercy are chasing after you to bring you closer to the Good Shepherd.

Notes

GREEN PASTURES

Day 28

SURROUNDED BY THE SHEPHERD'S LOVE.

Surely goodness and mercy shall follow me all the days of my life. PSALM 23:6

Remember, David has already said that the Good Shepherd leads His sheep: "He leads me beside still waters... He leads me in paths of righteousness for His name's sake" (23:2-3).

So, the Shepherd is in front of the sheep. But now he says that the Shepherd's goodness and mercy follow the sheep. So, in Christ, you are encircled in the love of Christ.

There is an ancient Celtic hymn attributed to St Patrick in the fifth century. It begins with these words, "I bind unto myself today, the strong name of the Trinity." Then it says:

> *Christ be with me, Christ within me,*
> *Christ behind me, Christ before me,*
> *Christ beside me, Christ to win me,*
> *Christ to comfort and restore me,*
> *Christ beneath me, Christ above me,*
> *Christ in quiet, Christ in danger,*
> *Christ in hearts of all that love me,*
> *Christ in mouth of friend and stranger.*

When the Lord is your shepherd, you are surrounded on all sides by the goodness and mercy of God—behind me, before me, beside me, beneath me, above me. Friend, nothing can ever separate you from the love of God that is in Christ Jesus our Lord (Rom. 8:39).

And when you belong to the Good Shepherd, this will always be true of you. Jerry Bridges says this so well: *Your worst days are never so bad that you are beyond the reach of God's grace. And your best days are never so good that you are beyond the need of God's grace.*

Here we are, anxious about our world, our country, our families, ourselves, and who knows what the future holds? But of this you can be certain: Whatever the future holds, God's goodness and God's mercy will follow you all the days of your life.

Notes

GREEN PASTURES

Day 29

YOUR RELATIONSHIP WITH THE SHEPHERD IN HEAVEN

I shall dwell in the house of the LORD forever.
PSALM 23:6

David is looking beyond His days in this world. He already said, "Surely goodness and mercy shall follow me all the days of my life." And when he looks beyond the days of his life in this world, he sees what comes after: The joy of eternity in the immediate presence of the Lord.

What will that be like? The first thing to say is that it will be very different from life in this world. When you dwell in the house of the Lord, faith will be turned to sight, old battles will be over, old wounds will be healed, and God will wipe away all tears from your eyes.

You will see Christ in His glory. His kingdom will come. Death will be defeated. Evil will be overthrown. Heaven will come to earth and God will dwell with His people in a world of love where He will make everything new.

Dwelling in the house of the Lord will be incomparably better than the greatest joys any of us have known in this life. Your experience in heaven will be very different from your life in this world, but your relationship with Jesus will be the same.

When John is given a glimpse of what it will be like when all of God's redeemed people are gathered in His presence, he says, "They are before the throne of God, and serve him day and night in his temple… They shall hunger no more, neither thirst anymore; the sun shall not strike them, nor any scorching heat" (Rev. 7:15-16).

Then, he tells us this: "For the Lamb in the midst of the throne will be their shepherd, and he will guide them to springs of living water" (7:17). The relationship you have with Jesus in this world will continue forever. If He is your shepherd now, He will be your shepherd then.

Notes

GREEN PASTURES

Day 30

THE SHEPHERD WILL GUIDE US TO STREAMS OF LIVING WATER

The Lamb in the midst of the throne will be their shepherd. REVELATION 7:17

Why will any of us be in heaven? There's only one reason: The Good Shepherd came to seek and to save the lost. Here's what that means: The Shepherd became one with the sheep. He took our flesh. He came into our world. He shared our life. He became the Lamb: "The Lamb of God who takes away the sin of the world" (John 1:29).

> *Like a lamb that is led to the slaughter*
> *and like a sheep that before its shearers is silent,*
> *so he opened not his mouth* (Isa. 53:7).

But God raised Him up and exalted Him to the highest place. The Lamb of God is the Lion of Judah. He reigns. And He says, "I give my sheep eternal life. They will never perish, and no one will snatch them out of my hand" (John 10:28).

> *For the Lamb in the midst of the throne will be their shepherd,*
> *and he will guide them to springs of living water…*
> (Rev 7:17).

Here's why eternal life will never be dull. The Good Shepherd will always be leading you into something new. Heaven will be a world of fresh discoveries and new delights. And it will be Jesus Himself who leads you into them. Heaven will not be a world in which you meet Jesus and then go off to pursue your own thing. The Lamb will be your shepherd.

Jesus said to the Father:

> *"I desire that they also, whom you have given me, may be with me where I am, to see my glory that you have given me because you loved me before the foundation of the world"* (John 17:24).

When we are in the Father's house, Jesus' prayer will be answered. We will be with Him where He is and see His glory. And the Shepherd will guide us to streams of living water.

Notes

GREEN PASTURES

Day 31

WHAT IF THE LORD IS NOT YOUR SHEPHERD?

The LORD is my shepherd. PSALM 23:1

STILL WATERS

What is your position if the Lord is *not* your shepherd? What is your position if you choose to be your own shepherd? Your own god? What if you choose to be the captain of your own ship, the master of your own soul? Then your reality will be something like this:

> *I am my own shepherd*
> *And I will always want.*
> *Sin makes me restless:*
>
> *It keeps me from lying down in green pastures*
> *It leads me beside troubled waters.*
> *It ruins my soul.*
>
> *Sin leads me in paths of unrighteousness*
> *which I pursue for my own sake.*
>
> *When I walk through the valley of the shadow of death,*
> *I will have great fear,*
> *for sin will be with me:*
> *Its guilt and its shame will haunt me.*

> *Sin prepares a table before me in the presence of my friends. It promises much, but it always disappoints.*
> *And my cup is always empty.*
>
> *Surely judgment and condemnation will follow me all the days of my life, and I shall dwell in the house of the lost forever.*

Who wants to say that? And if that's where you are, why should you stay there? The Good Shepherd has come to seek and to save the lost. He gave Himself for you and He calls you to follow Him.

The greatest blessing you can know in life is to be wholly owned by the Son of God. When you can say, "The Lord is my shepherd," then you will also be able to say, "Surely goodness and mercy shall follow me all the days of my life, and I shall dwell in the house of the Lord forever."

Notes

Open the Bible™
with Pastor Colin Smith

Published by *Open the Bible*
PO Box 3454, Barrington, IL 60011
Email: info@openthebible.org
Website: www.openthebible.org

Printed in the United States of America